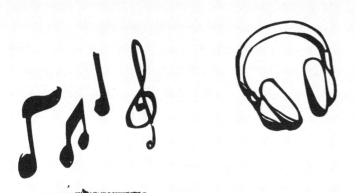

MY LIFE
JOURNAL

#VIRAL

Copyright © 2021 The Adventures of Pookie LLC
All rights reserved. This book or any portion thereof may not be reproduced or used in any manner whatsoever without the express written permission of the publisher except for the use of brief quotations in a book review.

For Bulk Order requests email: contact@adventuresofpookie.com

Printed in the United States of America
Paperback ISBN : 978-1-7365073-6-0

www.AdventuresOfPookie.com

HOW TO USE THIS JOURNAL

- **Pick a Special Spot to Journal**
Choose a time and place where you feel safe, happy, and secure and where you feel inspired to lose yourself in your journal writing.

- **Go with the Flow to Express Yourself**
Take some time and tune in to how you feel. Do you feel like writing a lot or simply feel like writing one word? When you go with the flow, your journal writing comes easily and feels great.

- **Silence Your Inner Critic**
It's your journal and your words and however you write them down they are valuable, NO MATTER WHAT!

- **Keep it Fun and Fulfilling**
If your journal writing begins to feel like a task you must accomplish, scale back or take a break. Just remember that your journaling experience is always more enjoyable when it feels spontaneous.

- **Create your avatar**
Use the guide in the back to create your avatar and design your life. Set goals and map out a plan to live your best life.

ALL ABOUT ME

I AM GOOD AT:

MY FAVORITE FOOD IS:

MY FAVORITE COLOR IS:

SOMETHING I WANT TO LEARN:

WHAT MAKES ME UNIQUE:

Circle the sentences that describe you.
Underline those that you would like to be.

i AM FUNNY.

i AM COMPASSIONATE.

i AM CALM.

i AM COURAGEOUS.

i AM POSITIVE.

i CARE FOR THE EARTH.

i AM MENTALLY TOUGH.

CHALLENGES HELP ME GROW.

i AM KIND.

i AM CONFIDENT.

i AM GRATEFUL.

i AM FOCUSED.

i AM WISE.

i AM ORGANIZED.

i COMMUNICATE WELL.

i AM INCLUSIVE.

i AM HOPEFUL.

BELIEVE IN THE POWER OF YOURSELF!

The more you practice, the better you will be at anything you want!

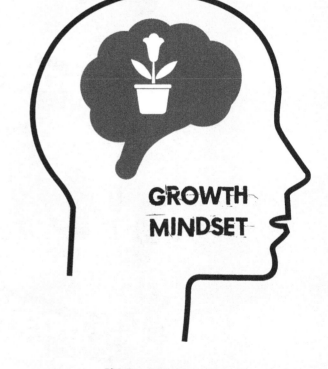

I'M NOT GOOD AT THIS.

I CAN'T DO THIS.

THIS IS TOO HARD.

I'LL TRY!

I'M RIGHT ON TRACK.

MISTAKES HELP ME LEARN.

POSITIVE *mind*

POSITIVE *vibes*

POSITIVE *life*

A **GOOD LIFE** comes from having the **right attitude** and taking the **right actions**.

Here a few things that make life great:

- having fun
- enjoying the love of family and friends
- doing things that you love to do
- becoming all that you can be
- helping others
- enjoying each moment

WHAT ARE SOME THINGS THAT MAKE YOUR LIFE GREAT?

_____
_____
_____
_____
_____
_____
_____
_____

DATE _____

DO I HAVE A FIXED MINDSET OR A GROWTH MINDSET? WHAT WILL I DO TO IMPROVE MY GROWTH MINDSET?

HOW DID I FEEL TODAY?

Angry   Sad   Meh   Okay   Happy   Excited

WHAT MADE ME FEEL THIS WAY?

_____
_____
_____
_____
_____
_____
_____
_____
_____
_____

DATE _____

WHAT ARE FIVE THINGS I AM REALLY GOOD AT? HOW CAN I IMPROVE AND BECOME BETTER AT THESE THINGS?

_____
_____
_____
_____
_____
_____
_____
_____
_____
_____
_____
_____
_____
_____
_____

HOW DID I FEEL TODAY?

Angry   Sad   Meh   Okay   Happy   Excited

WHAT MADE ME FEEL THIS WAY?

_____
_____
_____
_____
_____
_____
_____
_____
_____
_____
_____

DATE _____

WHEN WAS THE LAST TIME I WAS INTENTIONALLY KIND TO SOMEONE? WHAT WAS THEIR REACTION AND HOW DID IT MAKE ME FEEL?

HOW DID I FEEL TODAY?

Angry   Sad   Meh   Okay   Happy   Excited

WHAT MADE ME FEEL THIS WAY?

_____

_____

_____

_____

_____

_____

_____

_____

_____

_____

DRAW OR WRITE DOWN YOUR BIGGEST DREAM.

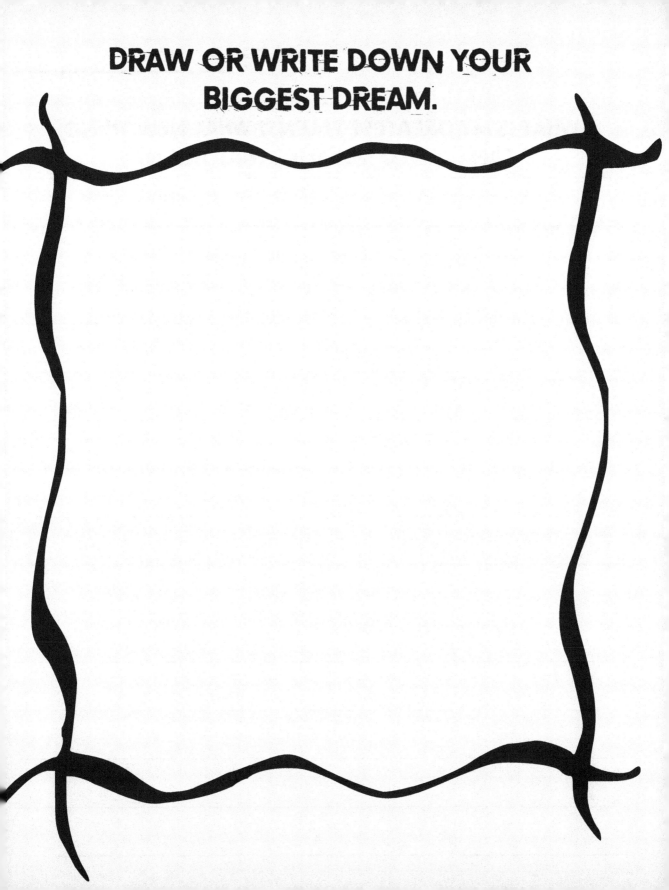

DATE _____

WHAT IS MY GREATEST TALENT? WHAT NEW THING CAN I TRY TO NURTURE THAT TALENT?

HOW DID I FEEL TODAY?

Angry   Sad   Meh   Okay   Happy   Excited

WHAT MADE ME FEEL THIS WAY?

_____
_____
_____
_____
_____
_____
_____
_____
_____
_____
_____

DATE _____

WHAT IS SOMETHING I GAVE UP ON? WOULD I TRY IT AGAIN? WHAT WOULD I DO DIFFERENTLY?

_____
_____
_____
_____
_____
_____
_____
_____
_____
_____
_____
_____
_____
_____
_____
_____
_____

HOW DID I FEEL TODAY?

Angry   Sad   Meh   Okay   Happy   Excited

WHAT MADE ME FEEL THIS WAY?

_____

_____

_____

_____

_____

_____

_____

_____

_____

_____

DATE _____

WHAT FEAR IS HOLDING ME BACK FROM ACCOMPLISHING A GOAL? HOW CAN I OVERCOME THAT FEAR?

_____
_____
_____
_____
_____
_____
_____
_____
_____
_____
_____
_____
_____
_____
_____

HOW DID I FEEL TODAY?

Angry   Sad   Meh   Okay   Happy   Excited

WHAT MADE ME FEEL THIS WAY?

_____
_____
_____
_____
_____
_____
_____
_____
_____
_____

Be yourself
EVERYONE ELSE
IS
ALREADY
taken

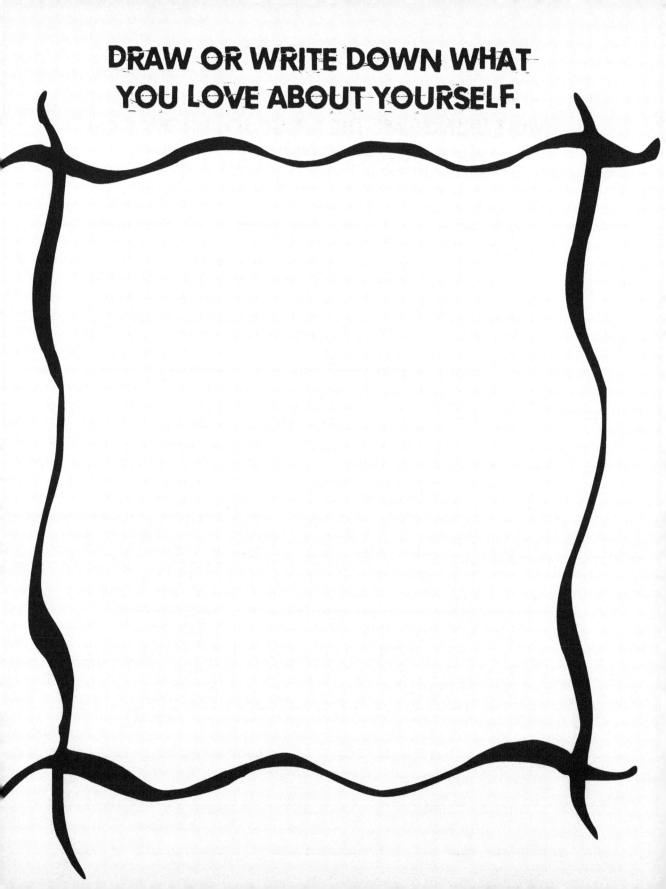

DATE _____

WHAT BRINGS ME THE MOST JOY? HOW CAN I HAVE MORE OF THAT IN MY LIFE?

HOW DID I FEEL TODAY?

Angry   Sad   Meh   Okay   Happy   Excited

WHAT MADE ME FEEL THIS WAY?

_____

_____

_____

_____

_____

_____

_____

_____

_____

_____

DATE _____

WHO IS THE PERSON IN MY LIFE THAT INSPIRES ME MOST? HOW CAN I THANK THEM FOR THAT INSPIRATION?

HOW DID I FEEL TODAY?

Angry   Sad   Meh   Okay   Happy   Excited

WHAT MADE ME FEEL THIS WAY?

_____
_____
_____
_____
_____
_____
_____
_____
_____
_____

DATE _____

WHAT IS SOMETHING I AM PASSIONATE ABOUT? HOW CAN I INFUSE SOME OF THAT PASSION INTO OTHER AREAS OF MY LIFE?

_____
_____
_____
_____
_____
_____
_____
_____
_____
_____
_____
_____
_____
_____
_____
_____
_____
_____
_____
_____
_____
_____

HOW DID I FEEL TODAY?

Angry   Sad   Meh   Okay   Happy   Excited

WHAT MADE ME FEEL THIS WAY?

_____

_____

_____

_____

_____

_____

_____

_____

_____

_____

What you do today can improve all your tomorrows

DRAW OR WRITE DOWN 5 THINGS YOU'RE GOOD AT.

DATE _____

HOW DO I FEEL ABOUT ASKING FOR HELP? WHAT NORMALLY HAPPENS WHEN I ASK FOR HELP? SHOULD I ASK FOR HELP MORE OFTEN?

HOW DID I FEEL TODAY?

Angry　　Sad　　Meh　　Okay　　Happy　　Excited

WHAT MADE ME FEEL THIS WAY?

_____
_____
_____
_____
_____
_____
_____
_____
_____
_____
_____
_____

DATE _____

WHEN I MAKE A MISTAKE, WHAT DOES MY INNER VOICE TELL ME? WHAT DO I WANT THAT VOICE TO SAY?

HOW DID I FEEL TODAY?

Angry   Sad   Meh   Okay   Happy   Excited

WHAT MADE ME FEEL THIS WAY?

_____
_____
_____
_____
_____
_____
_____
_____
_____
_____

DATE _____

HOW DO I DEFINE SUCCESS? DO I CONSIDER MYSELF SUCCESSFUL? WHY OR WHY NOT?

HOW DID I FEEL TODAY?

Angry Sad Meh Okay Happy Excited

WHAT MADE ME FEEL THIS WAY?

_____
_____
_____
_____
_____
_____
_____
_____
_____
_____
_____
_____

Believe in impossible

WHAT IS YOUR SUPERPOWER? DRAW OR WRITE IT HERE.

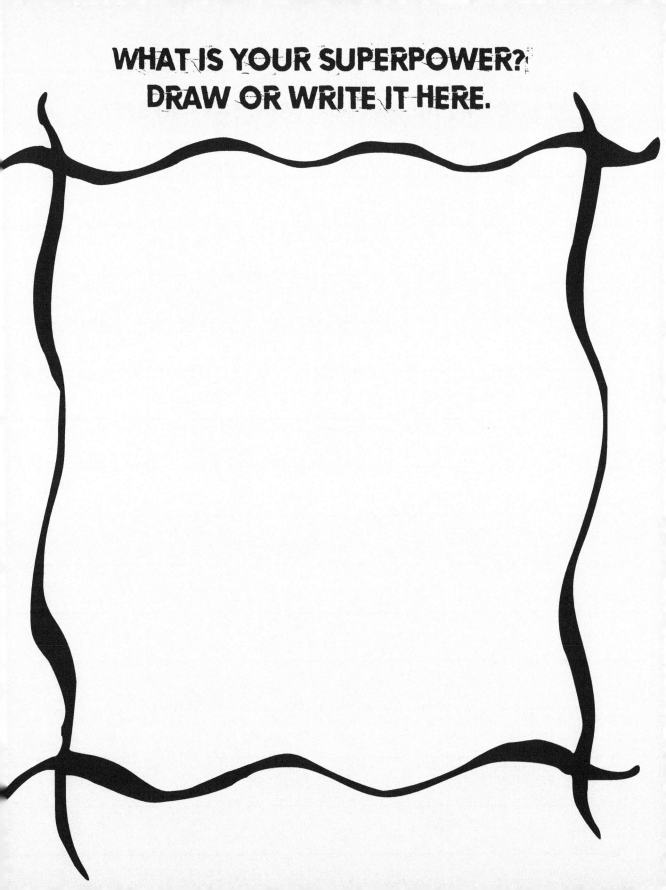

DATE _____

LOOK IN THE MIRROR. WHAT DO YOU SEE?

Think beyond physical features. For example: I see someone who is standing tall and looking confident. I see someone who is always smiling.

_____
_____
_____
_____
_____
_____
_____
_____
_____
_____
_____
_____
_____

HOW DID I FEEL TODAY?

Angry   Sad   Meh   Okay   Happy   Excited

WHAT MADE ME FEEL THIS WAY?

_____

_____

_____

_____

_____

_____

_____

_____

_____

_____

DATE _____

WHAT IS A LONG-TERM GOAL I HAVE SET FOR MYSELF? WHAT WILL I DO TODAY TO GET CLOSER ACCOMPLISHING THAT GOAL?

_____

_____

_____

_____

_____

_____

_____

_____

_____

_____

_____

_____

_____

_____

_____

HOW DID I FEEL TODAY?

Angry   Sad   Meh   Okay   Happy   Excited

WHAT MADE ME FEEL THIS WAY?

_____
_____
_____
_____
_____
_____
_____
_____
_____
_____
_____

DATE _____

WHAT AM I STRUGGLING WITH RIGHT NOW? IF SOMEONE ELSE WERE FACING THAT STRUGGLE, WHAT ADVICE WOULD I GIVE THEM?

_____

_____

_____

_____

_____

_____

_____

_____

_____

_____

_____

_____

_____

_____

HOW DID I FEEL TODAY?

Angry   Sad   Meh   Okay   Happy   Excited

WHAT MADE ME FEEL THIS WAY?

_____
_____
_____
_____
_____
_____
_____
_____
_____
_____
_____

Try & Fail
BUT NEVER
fail to
try

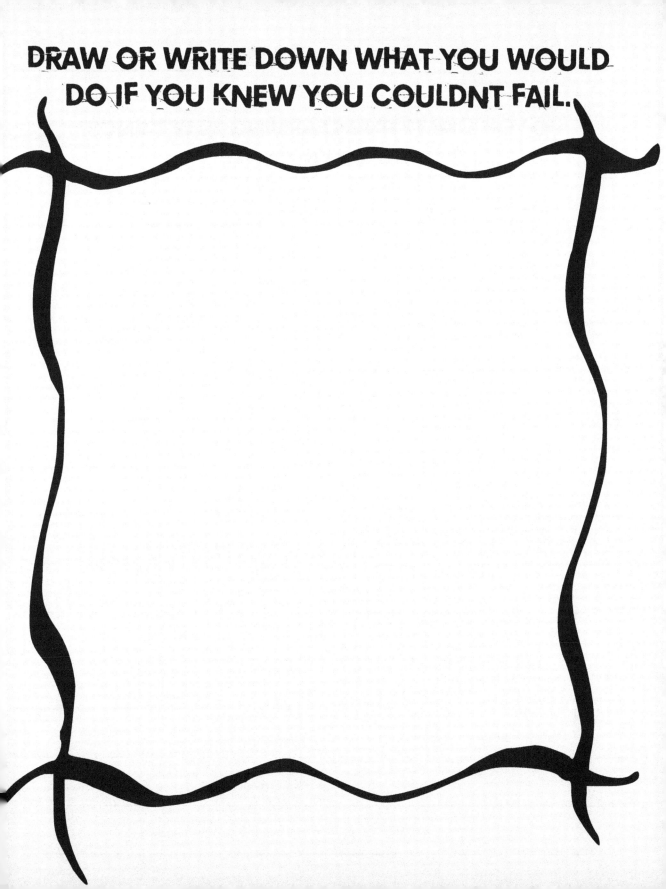

DATE _____

DO YOU LIKE TRYING/LEARNING NEW THINGS? WHY OR WHY NOT?

HOW DID I FEEL TODAY?

Angry   Sad   Meh   Okay   Happy   Excited

WHAT MADE ME FEEL THIS WAY?

_____
_____
_____
_____
_____
_____
_____
_____
_____
_____
_____

DATE _____

IF YOU COULD DO SOMETHING THAT YOU NEVER HAVE DONE BEFORE, WHAT WOULD IT BE? WHY WOULD YOU WANT TO DO IT?

_____
_____
_____
_____
_____
_____
_____
_____
_____
_____
_____
_____
_____
_____
_____
_____
_____

HOW DID I FEEL TODAY?

Angry   Sad   Meh   Okay   Happy   Excited

WHAT MADE ME FEEL THIS WAY?

_____
_____
_____
_____
_____
_____
_____
_____
_____
_____
_____

DATE _____

WHAT DOES CONFIDENCE FEEL LIKE? COMPARE THE FEELING TO SOMETHING ELSE, USING AS MUCH DETAIL AS POSSIBLE.

_____
_____
_____
_____
_____
_____
_____
_____
_____
_____
_____
_____
_____
_____
_____
_____
_____

HOW DID I FEEL TODAY?

Angry   Sad   Meh   Okay   Happy   Excited

WHAT MADE ME FEEL THIS WAY?

_____
_____
_____
_____
_____
_____
_____
_____
_____
_____
_____
_____

LIFE IS 10% WHAT happens TO YOU and 90% HOW YOU React TO IT

DATE _____

HOW DO I FEEL ABOUT CHANGE? HOW CAN I TURN CHANGE INTO OPPORTUNITY?

HOW DID I FEEL TODAY?

Angry   Sad   Meh   Okay   Happy   Excited

WHAT MADE ME FEEL THIS WAY?

_____

_____

_____

_____

_____

_____

_____

_____

_____

_____

DATE _____

HAVE YOU EVER BEEN AFRAID TO DO SOMETHING, BUT DID IT ANYWAY? WHAT WAS IT?

_____
_____
_____
_____
_____
_____
_____
_____
_____
_____
_____
_____
_____
_____
_____
_____

HOW DID I FEEL TODAY?

Angry   Sad   Meh   Okay   Happy   Excited

WHAT MADE ME FEEL THIS WAY?

_____
_____
_____
_____
_____
_____
_____
_____
_____
_____
_____

DATE _____

WHAT ARE YOU MOST GRATEFUL FOR IN YOUR LIFE? LIST AT LEAST 10 THINGS. CHOOSE 1 AND WRITE WHY YOU ARE GRATEFUL FOR IT.

HOW DID I FEEL TODAY?

Angry   Sad   Meh   Okay   Happy   Excited

WHAT MADE ME FEEL THIS WAY?

_____
_____
_____
_____
_____
_____
_____
_____
_____

Best things in life ARE free

DATE _____

WHAT DOES YOUR DREAM LIFE LOOK LIKE? DESCRIBE IT IN DETAIL.

_____
_____
_____
_____
_____
_____
_____
_____
_____
_____
_____
_____
_____
_____
_____

HOW DID I FEEL TODAY?

Angry

Sad

Meh

Okay

Happy

Excited

WHAT MADE ME FEEL THIS WAY?

_____
_____
_____
_____
_____
_____
_____
_____
_____
_____
_____
_____

DATE _____

WHAT DOES HAPPINESS MEAN TO YOU?

_____
_____
_____
_____
_____
_____
_____
_____
_____
_____
_____
_____
_____
_____
_____

HOW DID I FEEL TODAY?

Angry Sad Meh Okay Happy Excited

WHAT MADE ME FEEL THIS WAY?

_____
_____
_____
_____
_____
_____
_____
_____
_____
_____
_____

DATE _____

WHAT MAKES YOU FEEL ALIVE? AND WHEN WAS THE LAST TIME YOU FELT THAT WAY?

_____
_____
_____
_____
_____
_____
_____
_____
_____
_____
_____
_____
_____
_____
_____
_____
_____
_____

HOW DID I FEEL TODAY?

Angry   Sad   Meh   Okay   Happy   Excited

WHAT MADE ME FEEL THIS WAY?

_____
_____
_____
_____
_____
_____
_____
_____
_____
_____

life
is a
song
sing it

IF YOU COULD BE FAMOUS FOR ONE THING, WHAT WOULD IT BE? DRAW OR WRITE IT HERE.

DATE _____

SET A 2 MINUTE TIMER AND WRITE DOWN WHATEVER COMES TO YOUR MIND.

HOW DID I FEEL TODAY?

Angry   Sad   Meh   Okay   Happy   Excited

WHAT MADE ME FEEL THIS WAY?

_____

_____

_____

_____

_____

_____

_____

_____

_____

_____

DATE _____

WHAT DO YOU WISH YOUR PARENTS KNEW ABOUT YOU? WHAT DO YOU WISH YOUR FRIENDS OR CLASSMATES KNEW ABOUT YOU?

_____
_____
_____
_____
_____
_____
_____
_____
_____
_____
_____
_____
_____
_____
_____
_____
_____
_____

HOW DID I FEEL TODAY?

Angry   Sad   Meh   Okay   Happy

WHAT MADE ME FEEL THIS WAY?

_____
_____
_____
_____
_____
_____
_____
_____
_____
_____

DATE _____

DO I MAINLY THINK ABOUT THE PAST, PRESENT OR FUTURE? HOW CAN I BETTER BALANCE BEING PRESENT IN THE MOMENT WHILE ALSO PLANNING FOR THE FUTURE?

HOW DID I FEEL TODAY?

Angry   Sad   Meh   Okay   Happy

WHAT MADE ME FEEL THIS WAY?

_____
_____
_____
_____
_____
_____
_____
_____
_____
_____

it may **not be** easy but it will be **worth** it

A **GOOD LIFE** comes from having the **right attitude** and taking the **right actions**.

Use the following pages to design your life. Here are a few tips:

- Have fun with this activity!
- You can do anything you want with your life, so why not create something you want? Dream big!
- Think about who you are now, who you want to be, and what would make you happy.
- Don't be afraid. If you don't know how to do something yet, that is okay! You can always learn!
- START HERE:

WHAT DO YOU LIKE ABOUT YOURSELF?

_____
_____
_____
_____
_____
_____
_____
_____

CREATE YOUR AVATAR

Write down the type of person you wish you could be.

WHAT IS THEIR PERSONALITY?

_____
_____
_____
_____
_____

WHERE DO THEY WORK AND LIVE?

_____
_____
_____
_____
_____

HOW DO THEY REACT TO DIFFICULT SITUATIONS?

_____
_____
_____
_____
_____

WHAT DO THEY LIKE TO DO FOR FUN?

_____
_____
_____
_____
_____
_____

WHAT MAKES THEM DIFFERENT?

_____
_____
_____
_____
_____
_____

WHAT ARE THEIR CORE VALUES AND BELIEFS?

_____
_____
_____
_____
_____
_____
_____
_____

DESIGN YOUR LIFE – GOAL SETTING

Now that you have thought a little bit about the person you wish to become, let's figure out how you can make it happen.

Setting goals is not as complicated as it seems. Once you put it into practice, you will be able to set realistic goals and plan how to achieve them.

Goals should be SMART.

 – Specific

 – Measurable

 – Achievable

 – Rewarding

 – Time-bound

First, let's try setting a goal for something you want to accomplish this year.

Things to consider:
- What is one thing you want to get better at?
- What is something you want to try?
- How do you think you can make your talents grow?
- What other talents would you like to develop?
- What challenges seem to arise again and again?

MY GOAL

_____

_____

WHY DO I WANT TO ACHIEVE THIS GOAL?

_____

_____

To make a goal specific and measurable, you must answer 5 questions:

Who is involved?
_____

What do I want to accomplish?
_____

Where is it going to be achieved?
_____

When do I want to achieve it?
_____

How will you know you achieved it?
_____

DESIGN YOUR LIFE - GOAL SETTING

Now that you have defined exactly what you want to accomplish and made sure it is achievable, it's time to focus on the process to reach there.

BREAK IT DOWN INTO MINI-GOALS

Example: *I will collect $1000 for the local dog shelter within 6 months.*

MINI-GOAL 1: Sell cookies door-to-door around the neighborhood and collect $150.

MINI-GOAL 2: Set up a car wash with your friends and collect $300.

MINI-GOAL 3: Host a charity potluck and collect $300. Ask for volunteers around your neighborhood to help out by bringing dishes.

MINI-GOAL 4: Organize a scavenger hunt and charge a registration fee. Offer extra hints in exchange for additional donations. Collect $250.

BREAK DOWN MINI-GOALS INTO ACTION PLAN

MINI-GOAL 1: Sell cookies door-to-door

<u>Action Plan</u>:
- Calculate how many cookies I need to sell to reach my goal.
- Figure out what kind of cookies are more profitable to make and buy all the necessary ingredients.
- Bake the cookies with my parents and pack them into small containers.
- Offer cookies door-to-door.
- Calculate profit.

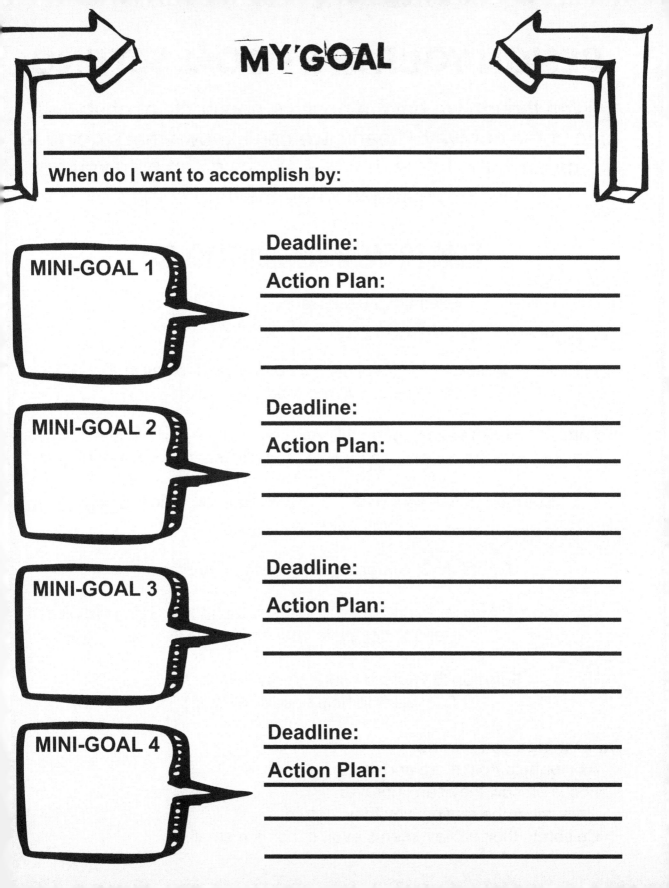

DESIGN YOUR LIFE – GOAL SETTING

Even though we have a positive perspective, obstacles can come our way. Clearly, we can't know what's going to happen in the future, but this exercise can help you get less discouraged when the time comes.

HOW TO OVERCOME OBSTACLES

Example: *I will collect $1000 for the local dog shelter within 6 months.*

Obstacle 1: *I don't have time to bake cookies in one week due to too much homework.*

Solution 1: Reschedule your deadlines. Just re-plan your deadlines so you can get your homework done on time, and still meet your 6 month goal.

Solution 2: Ask your mom, dad, grandma, or sibling to help you bake cookies.

Obstacle 2: *Struggling and feeling demotivated.*

Solution 1: Maybe you're pushing yourself too much. Set up smaller steps to complete your mini-goals.

Solution 2: Remind yourself why you set this goal. (You want to help needy animals.)

Other things you can do:
- Ask for help from mom and dad.
- Focus on how they can improve.
- Remember the reason why they started.
- Celebrate their achievements even if they are small.

OBSTACLES & SOLUTIONS

OBSTACLE 1

SOLUTION 1: _____
_____

SOLUTION 2: _____
_____

OBSTACLE 2

SOLUTION 1: _____
_____

SOLUTION 2: _____
_____

OBSTACLE 3

SOLUTION 1: _____
_____

SOLUTION 2: _____
_____

LOVE YOUR LIFE

Now get out there and **LIVE LIFE** to the fullest! You can do anything you want if you set your mind to it.

TIPS:
- Believe in yourself.
- Don't be afraid to try.
- Ask for help when you need it.
- Always have a positive mindset.

If you need extra goal setting pages, download them for free at AdventuresOfPookie.com

Made in United States
Orlando, FL
02 December 2022